I Can Draw!
MYTHICAL CREATURES

I CAN DRAW
MERMAIDS

JANE YATES

PowerKiDS
press

Published in 2018 by **The Rosen Publishing Group, Inc.**
29 East 21st Street, New York, NY 10010

Cataloging-in-Publication Data
Names: Yates, Jane.
Title: I can draw mermaids / Jane Yates.
Description: New York : PowerKids Press, 2018. | Series: I can draw!: mythical creatures | Includes index.
Identifiers: LCCN ISBN 9781538323489 (pbk.) | ISBN 9781538322529 (library bound) | ISBN 9781538323496 (6 pack)
Subjects: LCSH: Mermaids in art--Juvenile literature. | Animals, Mythical, in art--Juvenile literature. |
   Drawing--Technique--Juvenile literature.
Classification: LCC NC825.M9 Y38 2018 | DDC 743'.87--dc23

Developed and produced for Rosen by BlueApple*Works* Inc.

Creative Director: Melissa McClellan
Managing Editor for BlueApple*Works*: Melissa McClellan
Designer: T.J. Choleva
Photo Research: Jane Reid
Editor: Janice Dyer

Illustrations and Photo Credits: cover background Lotus_studio/Shutterstock; cover bottom right Semiankova Inha/Shutterstock; cover center Shafran/Shutterstock; cover top right New beginnings/Shutterstock; cover middle right Natasha_Chetkova/Shutterstock; cover top left Natasha_Chetkova/Shutterstock; title page, p. 6, 7, 8, 10, 11 Simon Streatfeild; TOC, p. 4 Lotus_studio/Shutterstock; p. 4 right E. S. Hardy/Creative Commons; p. 5 left, p. 5 middle Austen Photography; p. 5 left bottom domnitsky/Shutterstock; p. 5 bottom right Fotana/Shutterstock; p. 5 top right Coprid/Shutterstock; p. 5 top middle PhuShutter/Shutterstock; p. 9 SkyPics Studio/Shutterstock; p. 13 middle right aekikuis/Shutterstock; Simon Streatfeild p. 14–15, background image InnaVar/Shutterstock; Simon Streatfeild p. 16–17, background image PHOTOCREO Michal Bednarek/Shutterstock; Simon Streatfeild p. 26–27, background image rangizzz/Shutterstock; Simon Streatfeild p. 28–29, background image Jeremy Ryan/Shutterstock; Joshua Avramson; p. 18–19 final colored art, p. 19, Natasha_Chetkova/Shutterstock, background image Nanashiro/Shutterstock; Joshua Avramson; p. 20–21 final colored art, p. 21 New beginnings/Shutterstock, background image Ewais/Shutterstock; Joshua Avramson; p. 22–23 final colored art, p. 23 Natasha_Chetkova/Shutterstock, background image Nearbirds/Shutterstock; Joshua Avramson; p. 24–25 final colored art, p. 25 Shafran/Shutterstock, background image diversepixel/Shutterstock; Joshua Avramson; p. 30–31 final colored art, p. 31 Semiankova Inha/Shutterstock, background image Willyam Bradberry/Shutterstock

Manufactured in the United States of America
CPSIA Compliance Information: Batch BW18PK: For Further Information contact Rosen Publishing, New York, New York at 1-800-237-9932.

CONTENTS

MERMAIDS IN THE MYTHS

Mermaids are mythical creatures that are half-fish and half-human. They spend most of their time underwater. Cultures from all over the world tell stories of mermaids. It's thought that sightings of manatees and dugongs by early sailors may have been the original inspiration behind these ancient tales. Even the famous explorer Christopher Columbus claimed to have seen mermaids on his journeys!

Mermaids are known for their great beauty. Above the waist they commonly look like a beautiful woman with flowing hair. From the waist down they are like a fish with a graceful, long tail, ending in two fins. Myths claim that mermaids also have lovely singing voices.

In modern myth, mermaids are shown as kind beings who sometimes bring good fortune to people by granting them wishes. In some tales, they even marry and live with people. Probably the most famous of these is the fairy tale *The Little Mermaid*, by Hans Christian Andersen, which was the inspiration for the Disney film of the same name. However, the ancient tales of mermaid mythology tell a different story. A mermaid's enchanting voice is said to be able to lure ships onto rocks, sending sailors to their deaths.

So, are mermaids good or bad? It depends on which story you believe.

GET READY TO DRAW

Part of the fun of drawing is the huge variety of materials and techniques you can use. However, when you're getting started, it's usually best to start simple. Beginning artists have used pencils, pens, and paper for generations. If you have an art supply store near you, the staff there can usually recommend good starting equipment. They might even have starter kits you can buy. One invaluable piece of equipment is a sketchbook, a big book filled with blank pages. You can fill a sketchbook with practice drawings, and it can be fun to go back and see how you've improved.

Once you get the basics of putting pencil to paper, you'll want to start inking your drawings. Inking is when you go over the initial pencil marks with pen, which can help give your drawings a more finished look. Another piece of equipment that many artists begin using more once they get a little better is the eraser. Unlike the eraser at the end of your pencil, artists' erasers come in a variety of shapes and have a variety of uses. Some are just for getting rid of mistakes, while others help with advanced techniques like shading.

The core of a pencil is made of graphite, which is what makes a mark. Drawing pencils come in sets with different levels of graphite hardness. The softer the graphite, the darker a mark it makes.

There are tons of different types of drawing paper, and they all have different purposes. Tracing paper is very light, and is great for copying examples to see how to draw them.

Pens, like pencils, also come in different thicknesses. You can buy them in sets, and different sets might be recommended for different styles of drawing.

Different coloring tools have different feels, and it will take some **experimentation** to figure out what you like best. Colored pens, pencils, and markers are all great places to start.

Sharp corners on erasers can help create nice defined edges.

CARTOON STYLE DRAWING

Cartooning is a style many artists start out with. Because cartoons don't need to be realistic, it can be an easier style to get started with. With cartoons, an artist can provide a lot of information with just a few simple lines. A great place to begin is drawing faces. It's amazing how much can be shown through facial expressions! First, draw an oval to represent the head. Then, mark a cross, or t-shape, in the middle of the oval. This cross will help guide where to place facial features like the eyes, a nose, and a mouth.

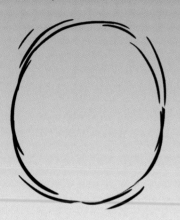

Draw an oval (or egg).

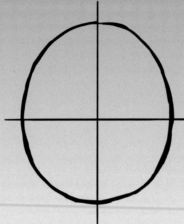

Divide the oval into four sections with two crossed lines.

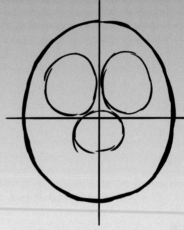

Draw three more ovals — two upright for the eyes, and one on its side for the nose.

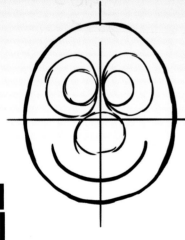

Draw two more ovals or circles for pupils, and a curved line for the mouth. Curved up is a smile and curved down is a frown.

Erase the cross and fill in the pupils. Add a few lines for hair, too.

Two more ovals work well for ears, and a few dots for freckles help give your cartoon some personality.

Once you know the basics of drawing a face, you can start experimenting. You can keep your cartoons simple, or you can make them more complex. Eyes can be two dots, or they can be huge, expressive shapes. You can use simple lines for mouths and eyebrows, but their placement can show a wide variety of emotions. Or you can exaggerate them with different shapes, sizes, and **textures**. A nose might just be a curved line, or it might be so big you can count individual nose hairs. There's no one right way to draw cartoons.

Eyebrows can show a huge variety of emotions.

Are they big, fuzzy, and out of control?

Or are they slim and shocked?

Even simple lines can add a lot to your drawings!

Once you know how to draw a face, it's time to think about other features. How does your character wear their hair? Whatever their style, remember, you don't have to worry about every little hair. You can draw an outline, and people will understand. You can also fill in the outline with a few line strokes to give the appearance of texture. You can use these same techniques for facial hair like beards and mustaches. A few dots can give the appearance of rugged **stubble**.

If you were a hairstylist, what look would best suit your character? Maybe some wild curls?

Or maybe your character has gone bald. What might that say about their personality?

Long, floppy hair can give a laid-back impression.

Spiky hair goes everywhere!

What kind of ears suit your character?

Adding a Y is an easy way to show the inside of the ears.

Use letters to shape your ears. You can use a C down low.

Or use an A up high!

CARTOON STYLE BODY SHAPE

When you begin drawing cartoon bodies, it's best to work with basic shapes. Simplicity is key. A popular shape that many artists use for bodies is a pear shape. One thing to remember is to try to avoid straight lines. These can look static and lifeless. Cartoons are supposed to be fun, and curvy, round bodies can give a feeling of playfulness.

Start with an oval for the head, and put it on top of a pear shape. Don't forget two circles for eyes.

Use slightly curved lines for the arms and legs. These look more natural than straight ruler lines would look.

Add some smoothed ovals for the hands and feet. Connect your head to your body with a neck before the head can float away!

On top of this, you can add clothes and other details like hair.

Good shapes to use when drawing characters are ovals, circles, and rounded rectangles. Try mixing and matching the shapes to best fit your character's outline.

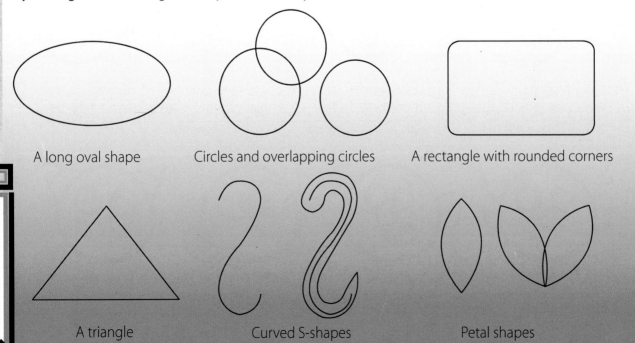

A long oval shape

Circles and overlapping circles

A rectangle with rounded corners

A triangle

Curved S-shapes

Petal shapes

REALISTIC STYLE DRAWING

You can draw more realistic looking characters using the same shapes and forms as you do with cartoon characters. However, now that you know how to define the forms, it will help if you outline a simple skeleton structure using lines. They will guide you by showing the character's joints, such as elbows and knees, so you can draw your character in the position you want.

 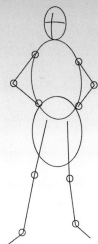 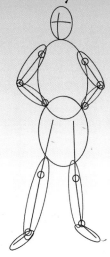

Use rounded shapes to outline the head and body of your character like you did before. Don't worry if it looks a little rough, you can always clean it up!

Now add some lines that are connected with circles where the joints would be for the arms and legs.

Add more oval shapes and lines to make an outline of the position of the body.

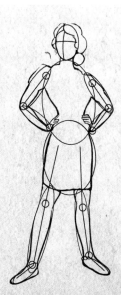  

Next, outline the arms and legs using the skeleton as a guide.

Finally, add details for the face and clothes.

Cool! You've got a finished character! Things like clothing and **accessories** can say a lot about your character. Can you tell your character's story with just a single image?

MANGA STYLE DRAWING

There are countless styles that a new artist can explore. From cartoons to photorealism, it's all a matter of what you enjoy drawing and looking at. One style that has proven extremely popular is manga. Manga started out as a style of Japanese comics, but today its popularity has spread all over the world. Some popular examples of manga include Sailor Moon and Dragon Ball Z. Animated cartoons that are based on manga are called anime.

Characters in manga are famous for having large eyes that can express a lot. In contrast, most of their other facial features are usually pretty simple. However, they tend to make up for this simplicity with their big, crazy hairstyles! Most manga characters have a few similarities, but like other styles of art, each artist has their own way of doing things.

MANGA STYLE EYES

In manga, eyes are one of the most noticeable features. They tend to be large, and can show a variety of emotions.

MANGA STYLE HAIR

Manga-style hair is also immediately recognizable. It's often spiky and wild, and totally impossible to pull off in real life!

First, make a general outline of your character's hair. Then add some strands in different sizes and shapes.

Usually hair all flows out from a single point on the top of the head, but you might want to experiment with different approaches.

MANGA STYLE BODIES

Manga bodies tend to be more realistic than cartoons. Start with an oval for the head and rectangles for the body. For limbs, you can use the skeleton techniques you learned on page 9. Look at other examples of manga for inspiration for manga style poses.

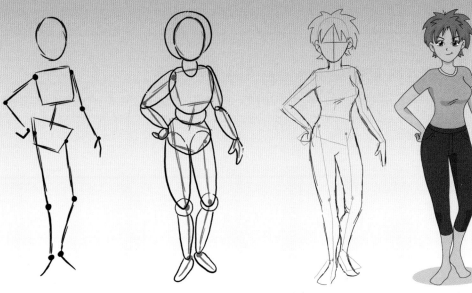

Start by drawing lines to show the figure. Draw small circles to show the joints.

Add ovals and rectangular shapes to outline the shape of the body.

Use a thicker pencil to draw the final outline of the character. Start adding some details, like hair.

Erase the guidelines and color the final shape. Add facial features and other details.

FINISHING YOUR DRAWINGS—INKING

Once you're done drawing, erase all your guidelines and everything else you don't want in the final version. You can erase these lines one step at a time as you go, or all at once at the end. You can also go over your drawing in pencil again to make the lines bolder. Once you're done with a pencil drawing, you can also go over your lines with a pen. This process is called inking.

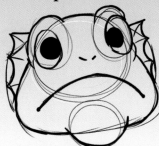

Complete your drawing.

Erase all extra lines that you used to create your character.

Go over your drawing again with a thicker pencil, or with an inking pen.

COLORING YOUR DRAWINGS

Most art looks just fine in black and white. However, many artists believe that color is the only way to really get their art to pop! If you feel the same way, there are a variety of tools and techniques you can use to achieve your desired effect. Pencils, crayons, and markers are great to get a feel for how coloring works. As you get better you might even want to try watercolor paints!

COLORING WITH PENCILS OR CRAYONS

Shading is a technique that helps create contrast between light and dark areas. First, figure out where your drawing's light source is. Is it above your character? Below it? This will help you to determine what is in shadow, and what is brightly lit. Well-lit areas will usually be brighter, while shadowy areas will be darker.

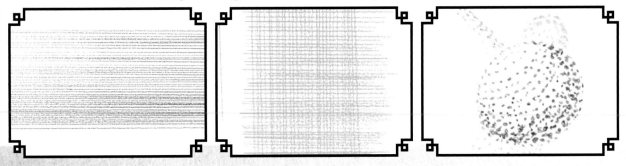

Hatching is a shading technique that uses lines that all go in the same direction.

Cross-hatching is just like hatching except you also add lines going in an opposite direction. This creates a richer texture in drawings.

Stippling is another shading technique, but instead of using lines, it uses dots. The more dots, the more shaded your subject looks.

COLORING WITH MARKERS

Markers are a great tool to use for coloring. They're simple, they don't need to be prepared in any way for use, and once the color is on the page, it dries fairly quickly. Because marker ink is liquid, it creates a smoother mark than pencils or crayons do.

Choose the colors you want to work with.

Fill in each separate section of your drawing, just like in a coloring book.

You can shade your drawing by using darker or lighter markers.

COLORING WITH WATERCOLORS

Watercolor paints come in tubes, or you can get multiple colors in a pan. The nice thing about using a pan is that you can remove the clear lid and use it as a watercolor palette. You can use the palette to mix together different colors to create new ones.

Choose the sections of your drawing you want to fill in with paint.

If you don't have the exact shade you want, try mixing colors together. Once you've got your desired color, fill in the rest of your drawing.

If you accidentally cover up some of your lines with paint, don't worry! Just wait for the paint to dry, and then go over the line again with pencil.

WORKING WITH COLORS

A color wheel is a tool that artists use to help understand colors. It shows what colors look like mixed together, and helps to give an idea of how different colors are related. It also shows which colors look good together, and which ones don't.

There are three types of colors on a color wheel: primary colors, secondary colors, and tertiary colors. Primary colors are blue, red, and yellow. These colors can't be made by mixing other colors together. Secondary colors are green, orange, and violet or purple. These colors can be made by mixing two primary colors together. For example, red and blue together make violet. Tertiary colors are made by mixing a primary color with a secondary color that's beside it on the color wheel.

COMPLEMENTARY COLORS

Colors that are located directly opposite from each other on the color wheel are considered complementary colors. That means they balance each other out. Primary colors are complemented by secondary colors. For example, orange complements blue, green complements red, and violet complements yellow. Using these colors together in a drawing can help create great looking art!

YELLOW
YELLOW GREEN
YELLOW ORANGE
GREEN
ORANGE
BLUE GREEN
RED ORANGE
BLUE
RED
BLUE VIOLET
RED VIOLET
VIOLET

P – Primary colors
S – Secondary colors
T – Tertiary colors

Yellow and blue are two neighboring primary colors. Mixing them together will create the secondary color green.

Blue and green are two neighboring primary and secondary colors. Mixing them together will create the blue-green tertiary color.

SWIMMING MERMAID

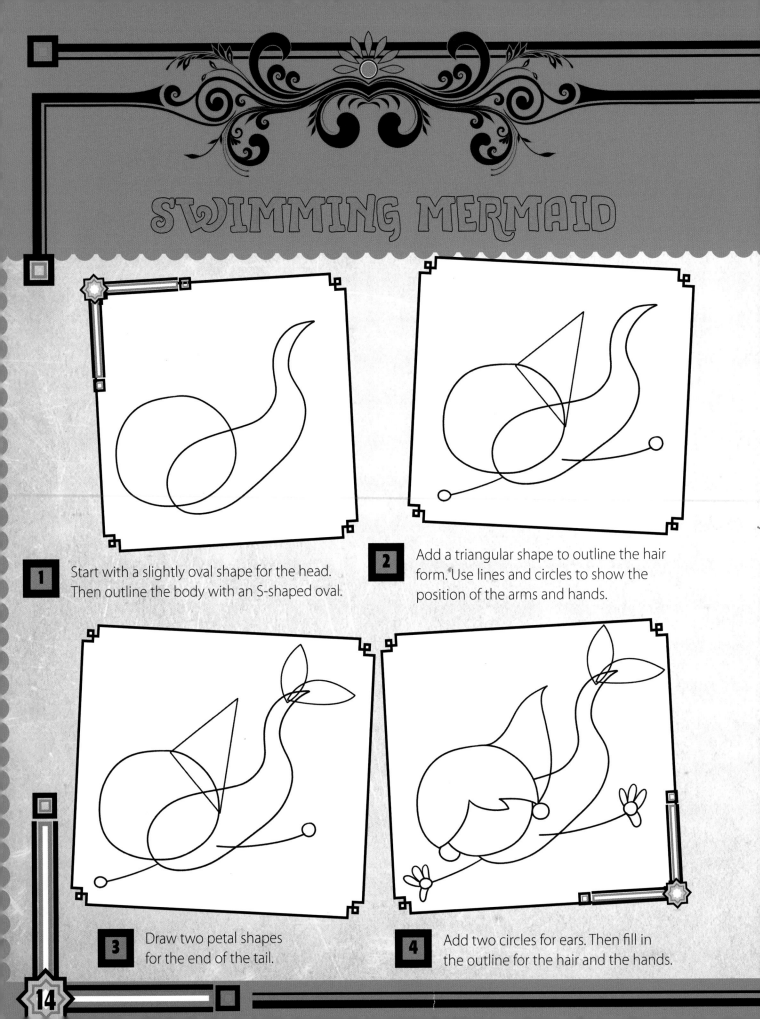

1 Start with a slightly oval shape for the head. Then outline the body with an S-shaped oval.

2 Add a triangular shape to outline the hair form. Use lines and circles to show the position of the arms and hands.

3 Draw two petal shapes for the end of the tail.

4 Add two circles for ears. Then fill in the outline for the hair and the hands.

5 Work on the arms by giving them a wider base. Add more details to the hair and finish outlining the tail fins.

6 Clean up the drawing by erasing your guidelines. Next, draw the facial features and add details to the tail.

7 Add final details to the face and ears. Draw a few scales on the fishtail part of your drawing. Then add a few bubbles.

8 To finish your mermaid, color the drawing.

HARP-PLAYING MERMAID

1 Start with a circle shape for the head.

2 Add three more overlapping oval shapes to outline the body. Draw two petal shapes for the tail fins.

3 Outline the arm by drawing three oval shapes. Then, outline the shape of the hair.

4 Draw the outline for the hair, then follow the shapes and draw a clean outline. Add a rectangular shape to outline the harp.

6 Clean up the drawing by erasing your guidelines. Then, start adding details. Draw clothes, and add a few more details to the harp.

5 Draw the facial features, then add details to the hair and the harp.

7 Add final details to the face. Draw a few scales on the fishtail part of your drawing. Then add a few bubbles and musical notes to show that the mermaid is playing her harp.

8 Color the drawing to finish your art project.

DANCING MERMAID

1 Start with a circle shape for the head. Add an oval shape to outline the body shape. Connect the two with another oval shape for the neck.

2 Add two long oval shapes to outline the arms.

3 Add two petal shapes for the tail.

4 Next, follow the shapes and draw a clean outline for the mermaid's body. Erase your guidelines.

5 Next, focus on the face. Draw the eyes, nose, ears, and smiling mouth. Don't forget the eyebrows.

6 Draw the mermaid's hair outline. Then, fill the shape with curvy lines to show strands of hair.

7 Fill in the details. Draw the clothes. Don't forget to draw scales and fin ridges for the fishtail part of your mermaid.

8 Color the drawing to finish your project.

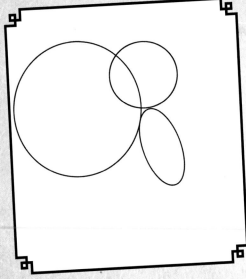

1 Draw an oval shape for the upper body and two overlapping circle shapes for the head and the hair.

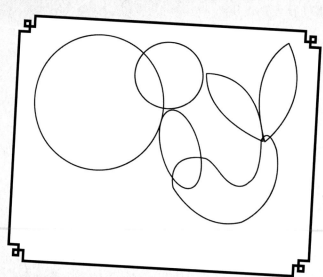

2 Now add an S-shaped overlapping oval for the bottom half and two petal shapes to outline the tail.

3 Add a line for the arms and small circles to show the joints.

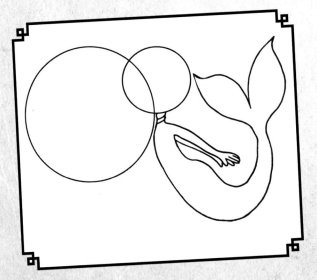

4 Next, follow the shapes and draw a clean outline for the mermaid's body. Erase your guidelines.

6 Focus on the head and hair. Draw the eye, pointy nose, ear, and pouty mouth. Then work on the hair, drawing curved lines to show floating strands.

5 Next, separate the tail part from the upper body part by drawing two pointy oval shapes.

7 Add final details such as the clothes, scales, and fin lines. Add more details to the hair to complete the drawing.

8 To finish your art, color the drawing. If you wish, cut it out and glue the drawing on a background image showing a mythical underwater world.

1 Start with a circle shape for the head. Add another oval shape to outline the body shape. Connect the two with another oval shape for the neck.

2 Add another overlapping oval shape to outline the hair.

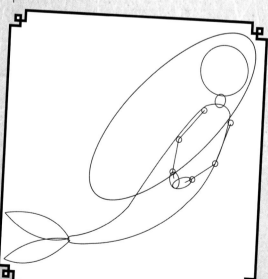

3 Add lines to outline the position for the arms and small circles to show the joints.

4 Next, follow the shapes and draw a clean outline for the mermaid's body. Erase your guidelines.

6 Next, draw the facial features. Draw simple eyes, eyebrows, a nose, and the mouth by drawing curved lines.

5 Finish outlining the mermaid's hair. Then, fill the shape with curvy lines to show strands of hair. Add the ears.

7 Add final details such as the clothes, scales, and fin lines.

8 Color the drawing to finish this dreamy mermaid. Don't forget to color two pink circles to show her rosy cheeks.

MERMAID PRINCESS

1 Start with an oval shape for the head. Add another oval shape to outline the body shape. Then add an overlapping S-shaped oval for the tail.

2 Add two crossed lines to outline the facial features as explained on page 6. Add two petal shapes to outline the tail.

3 Add lines and small circles to outline the position for the arms.

4 Next, follow the shapes and draw a clean outline for the mermaid's body. Erase your guidelines.

5 Add details to the hands by drawing fingers in place of the ovals. Then follow the crossed lines and draw the facial features.

6 Next, focus on the hair. Draw the hair outline going around and across the mermaid's body. Once done, fill the shape with curvy lines to show strands of hair. Then draw the tiara in her hair.

7 Add final details such as the scales and fin lines.

8 Color the drawing to finish your project.

SURPRISED MERMAID

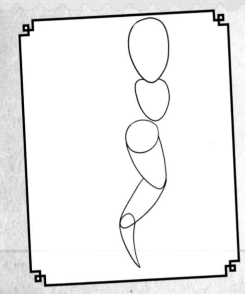

1 Outline the mermaid's shape by drawing a series of oval and circle shapes. Add a pointy oval for the end of the tail.

2 Add the lines for the arms and legs and small circles to show the joints.

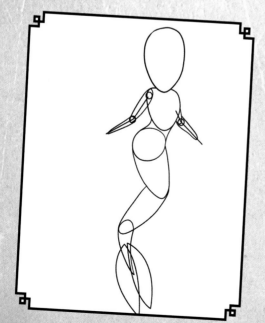

3 Add more oval shapes to outline the arms. Add two petal shapes for the tail.

4 Next, follow the shapes and draw a clean outline for the mermaid's body. Erase your guidelines.

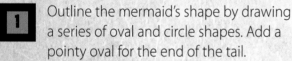

6 Add details to the face by filling in the eyes. Add ears and add curvy lines to the hair to show the strands.

5 Outline the hair, facial features, and clothes. Separate the upper body from the tail part by drawing a V-shaped line.

7 Add final details such as the clothes, scales, and fin lines. Add bubbles to complete your drawing.

8 Color the drawing to finish your art.

FROLICKING MERMAID

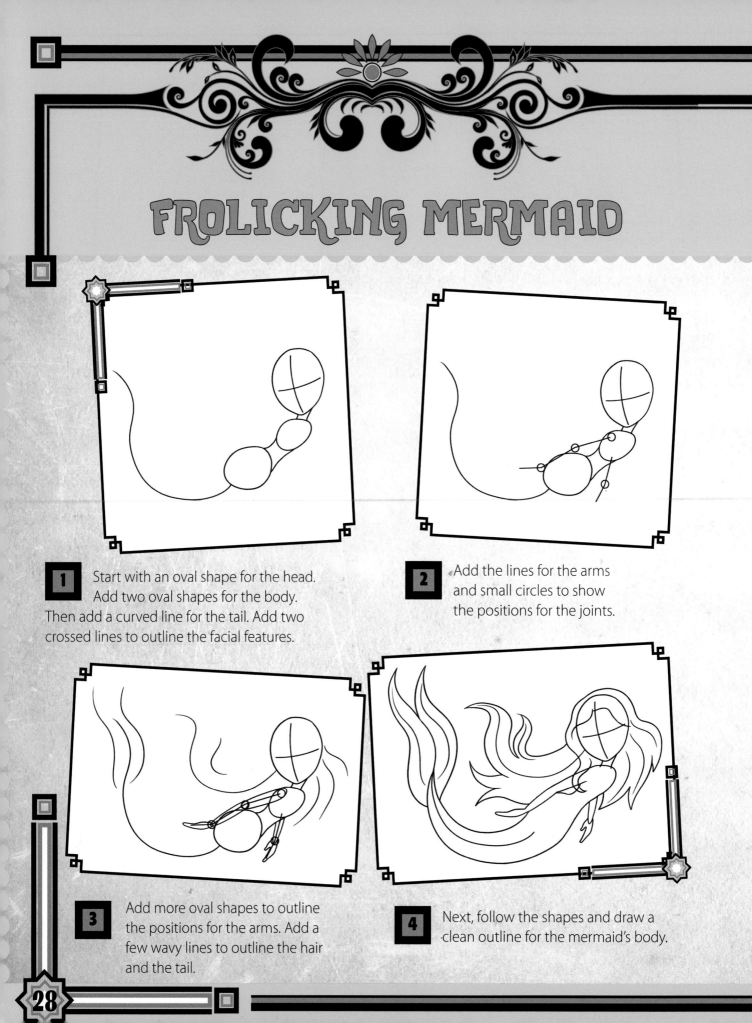

1 Start with an oval shape for the head. Add two oval shapes for the body. Then add a curved line for the tail. Add two crossed lines to outline the facial features.

2 Add the lines for the arms and small circles to show the positions for the joints.

3 Add more oval shapes to outline the positions for the arms. Add a few wavy lines to outline the hair and the tail.

4 Next, follow the shapes and draw a clean outline for the mermaid's body.

5 Erase your guidelines. Then follow the crossed lines and draw the facial features.

6 Add details to the facial features. Then, draw clothes and separate the upper body from the tail part by drawing a V-shaped line. Erase any lines you don't need.

7 Finish the drawing by adding the fin lines, a few scales, and a few more hair strands. Don't forget to draw big manga-style eyes.

8 To finish this happy mermaid, color the drawing.

ENCHANTING MERMAID

1 Start by outlining the mermaid's shape by drawing oval shapes. Add two petal shapes for the tail.

2 Add the lines for the arms and small circles to show the positions for the joints. Add two crossed lines to outline the facial features.

3 Next, follow the shapes and draw a clean outline for the mermaid's body. Erase your guidelines.

4 Add details to the hands by drawing fingers in place of the ovals. Add details to the tail fin.

5 Follow the crossed lines and draw the eyes, nose, and a small mouth.

6 Draw the mermaid's hair outline going around and behind her body. Once done, fill the shape with curvy lines to show strands of hair. Then draw the ribbon in her hair.

7 To finish this drawing, add details such as the clothes and scales.

8 Color the drawing to complete your art.

GLOSSARY

accessories Something added to something else to make it more attractive or effective.

dugong A large sea mammal that has flippers for front legs and a tail like a whale.

experimentation Testing to see how well something works.

invaluable Extremely useful.

lure Something that attracts or tempts.

manatee A gentle sea mammal that has flippers for front legs.

palette A board used to mix colors when painting.

photorealism A style of art that is realistic like a photograph.

static Does not change.

stubble A very short beard.

texture The feel or appearance of a surface.

FOR MORE INFORMATION

FURTHER READING

James, Elizabeth. *How To Draw for Kids*.
London, UK: Kyle Craig Publishing Ltd., 2016.

Legendre, Philippe. *I Can Draw Animals Around the World*.
Minneapolis, MN: Lerner Publications, 2015.

Santillan, Jorge, and Sarah Eason. *Drawing Fairies, Mermaids, and Unicorns*.
New York, NY: Gareth Stevens Publishing, 2014.

WEBSITES

PowerKids Press has developed an online list of websites related to the subject of this book. This site is updated regularly. Please use this link to access the list:
www.powerkidslinks.com/icd/mermaids

INDEX